DRAWING FASHION

A step-by-step guide to drawing fashion figures, clothes and fabrics

HILARY LOVELL

ARCTURUS

This edition published in 2011 by Arcturus Publishing Limited
26/27 Bickels Yard, 151–153 Bermondsey Street,
London SE1 3HA

ISBN: 978-1-84837-765-3
CH001683EN
Supplier 05, Date 0411, Print run 604

Illustrated by Hilary Lovell
Edited by Kate Overy
Designed by Dynamo Limited
Cover and additional design by Ariadne Ward

Printed in Singapore

CONTENTS

INTRODUCTION

In this book, fashion designer Hilary Lovell teaches you how to draw eighteen beautiful fashion models, taking inspiration from the catwalk and from classic design icons. Each section is broken down into clear, easy-to-follow drawing steps, so you can see your fashion models come to life.

Before you start creating your models, read the useful hints and tips in the opening section. You will find advice on which drawing tools to use and some helpful tips on how to elongate your model and ink and colour it in.

Look out for the special feature pages at the end of each chapter. These give you lots of ideas about how to put a collection together and ways to accessorize your model.

So now you can start putting pencil to paper and losing yourself in the fabulous world of fashion!

DRAWING TOOLS

Let's start by looking at the tools you'll need to create your fashion models. It's a good idea to invest in the essentials, then build up your collection of drawing tools over time.

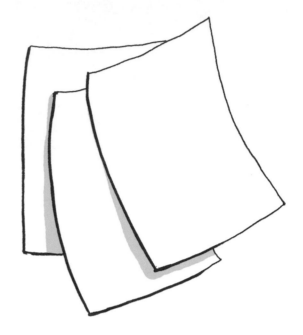

LAYOUT PAPER

There are so many different types of paper that it can be difficult to know which is best for your drawings. It's a good idea to start with a basic, inexpensive paper, such as layout paper, while you experiment with the different features of your characters. When you have a rough drawing you are happy with, you can move on to a heavier, higher-quality paper for your final version.

WATERCOLOUR PAPER

This type of paper is useful if you plan to colour your finished drawings using water-based paints. It is made from 100 per cent cotton and comes in a variety of weights and textures – 300 gsm (grams per square metre) or above is best.

CARTRIDGE PAPER

This top-quality paper is most frequently used for illustration and drawing and is ideal for your final version. You don't need to buy the most expensive brand to get great results.

PENCILS

Most of your work will be done in pencil, so it's a good idea to make sure you are comfortable with the type of pencil you choose. Graphite, or lead pencils come in different grades and are marked 'B' for blackness, or 'H' for hardness. '2H' is a good pencil to start with, as it leaves clean lines and few smudges. From here you can experiment with slightly blacker or harder pencils until you find one you are happy with. A lead holder pencil, or technical pencil is useful because you can draw thinner lines with this, and the lead breaks less frequently than with a traditional pencil.

ERASERS

Erasers come in three types: rubber, plastic and putty. All three are effective, but most people start with rubber erasers.

PENS

The most important thing to consider when choosing a pen is how you plan to colour your art. If you intend using water-based paints, then you need a waterproof ink pen. The nib thickness of most pens is marked on the lid, and usually ranges from 0.1 to 0.5. Nib thicknesses 0.2 or 0.3 are usually the best to work with. 0.1 is very fine, and good for inking tiny details on your model's outfit or face.

BRUSHES

Another way of inking your work is with a fine brush. This technique is quite difficult to master as it requires a very steady hand and a good-quality sable brush. Brushes are also great for adding glitter or sparkle details.

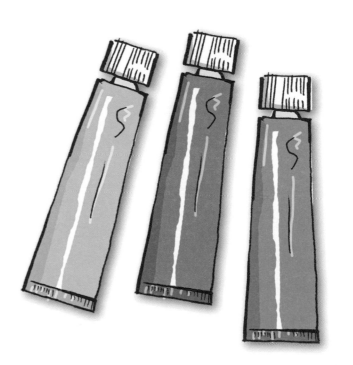

PAINTS

Most art stores stock a variety of paints, including acrylics, watercolours, oils and gouache. If you want to colour your characters by hand, it is best to experiment with different paints until you find one you are comfortable with.

COMPUTER SOFTWARE

Another option is to scan your inked illustrations on a computer and then colour them digitally. Software programs that let you create layers are useful for giving depth to your illustrations.

How to create your model

For fashion illustration, it's useful to learn the basics of drawing the human form. Flicking through a fashion magazine or just looking in the mirror will give you an idea of the body's structure.

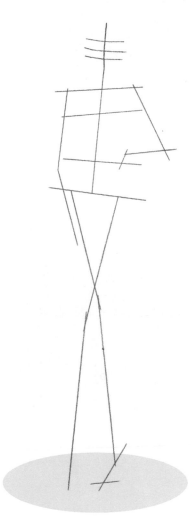

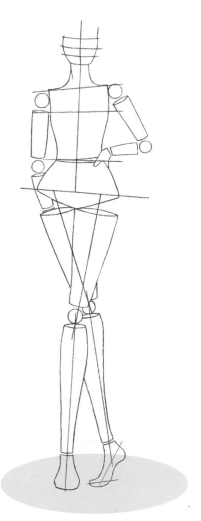

STEP 1 ▲

Start by drawing the basic frame of the body and a grid for the position of the facial features.

STEP 2 ▲

Build up your frame using basic shapes such as cylinders for the arms and legs, and spheres for the shoulder, elbow and knee joints. Draw a simple body shape for the torso.

STEP 3 ▲

When you are happy with your pencil drawing, it's time to bring your model to life by adding fine details, followed by ink and final colour.

Elongating your model

One of the secrets of fashion drawing is knowing how to elongate your model. Longer legs, arms, body and neck make the model look elegant and show off the clothes to their best advantage.

▼ STANDARD BODY

↑ Standard body is the same height as seven heads

▼ ELONGATED MODEL POSE

Elongate the neck, torso, arms and legs

↑ Elongated model pose is the same height as eight heads

Transparency

Gathered fabric

To show that a fabric such as organza or mesh has some transparency, you need to give an impression of the clothing or skin underneath. Achieve this by drawing it lightly, then colour it to show the effect of colours on top of each other. For instance, if you have yellow clothing under a blue organza, the yellow becomes a shade of green through the blue.

A good way to draw gathered fabric is to use a lot of lines in the direction of the gathers, whether they are around the waist of a skirt or the back of a dress. Use a thicker ink line to show shading and add more definition to the gathers.

Fabric creasing

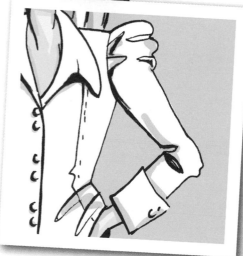

To show creasing, add more line detail in the places where the fabric gathers and creases, such as round the elbows and waist. Use a heavier ink line to add depth and enhance the look of the creasing.

Pleating

A good way to show pleats is to use a printed fabric. This tartan works well because you draw your pattern round the shape of the fabric. Pleating is a great way to illustrate movement too!

INKING TIPS

Don't worry if your pencil drawings are a bit messy and smudged to start with — sketching and building your figure can involve a lot of corrections! When your model is complete and you are happy with the drawing, it's time to start inking.

ORIGINAL PENCIL VERSION

Inking allows you to choose the best lines you have put down and make them stand out from the rest.

FINAL INK VERSION

Areas with lots of pencil shading become solid black when inked. These include the gathers of the skirt hem and the area under the jaw line.

After the inking stage, it's time to colour your model. Start by applying your base tones, then build up the colour by layering other shades on top. Experiment with pens, pencils and paints until you achieve the desired result.

STEP 1 ▶

Start by deciding on your colour scheme, then lay down your basic tones.

◀ STEP 2

Next, using darker tones of the base colours, add the shaded areas to your model.

STEP 3 ▶

Finally, add highlights to the areas where light would reflect, using whites and lighter shades of the base colours. Highlights to eyeshadow and lipstick give the make-up a glossy finish.

MODERN CLASSICS

Modern classics are an essential part of any fashionista's wardrobe. Understated and sophisticated, they feature prominently in fashion collections over and over again. Get drawing with these timeless pieces!

TRENCH COAT

The tightly-belted trench coat has been a fashion classic since the 1940s. Here it is updated in a shorter length with a flared cut, large lapels and buttons. Get into super sleuth mode with this gorgeous garment!

STEP 1 ▶

Draw your frame with soft lines, creating a relaxed standing pose. Keep the stance open to really show off the front of the jacket.

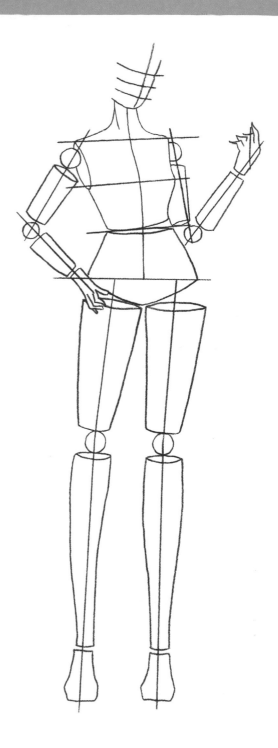

Create your body shape, using cylinders and balls to map out the limbs and torso.

Now build up the jacket, working it round the shape of the body. The tilted-back pose helps the coat flare out from the waist. An exaggerated collar gives a modern twist.

STEP 4 ▶

Now for the hairstyle. A simple, long bob sits well on the large collar. Originally trench coats were designed as raincoats and made from waterproof heavyweight cotton. Today they are made in a range of fabrics and are worn as fashion statements as well as protection from the rain!

STEP 5 ▶

Time to accessorize! A statement ring on the index finger and a patent leather shopper complete this classic look. The belt is tied in a knot, rather than buckled, for a casual feel.

TOP TIP
Shade around the buttons to add to the 3-D effect. This way they will look stitched on, rather than printed.

TOP TIP

Choose your model's skin tone carefully so it stands out against the light-coloured beige trench coat.

STEP 6 ▶

Start inking in your pencil. Use a thicker line around the collar and belt to make them stand out from the main part of the jacket.

STEP 7 ▶

Beige is the traditional colour for the trench coat. Add dark chocolate-brown accessories. Use lots of highlights to give the coat a slightly wet look and to create the appearance of patent leather.

LITTLE BLACK DRESS

No wardrobe is complete without this fashion staple. It's a versatile piece that can either be dressed up or down – however the mood takes you. Effortlessly chic, this flattering dress is suitable for any event.

◀ STEP 1

Create your frame using lines. Tilt the shoulders and head a little to make the pose less rigid.

STEP 2 ▶

Build up your body structure using the basic shapes over the frame lines.

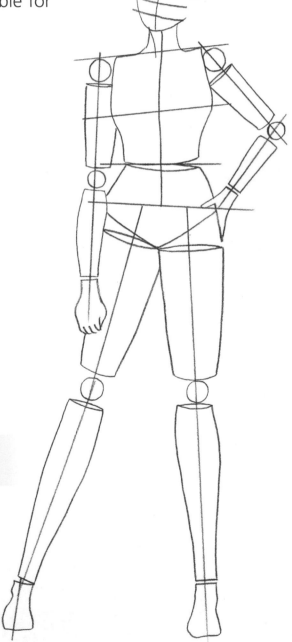

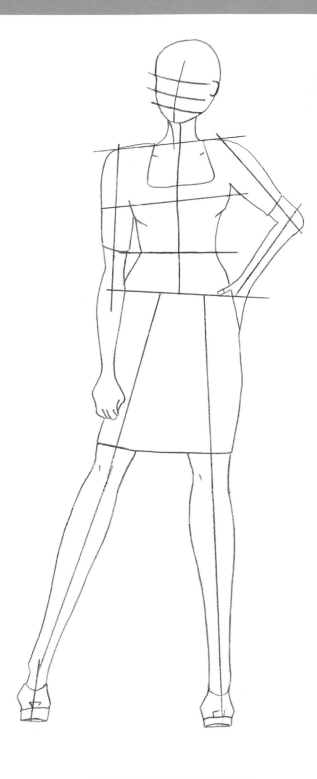

◀ **STEP 3**

Add the outline of the little black dress over the body shape. Keep the dress fitted to the model's body. To lengthen the legs and add height, draw some peep-toed wedged shoes.

STEP 4 ▶

Add the facial features and a layered, bobbed hairstyle. Keeping the hairstyle short helps show off the shape of the dress and the model's neckline.

MODERN CLASSICS

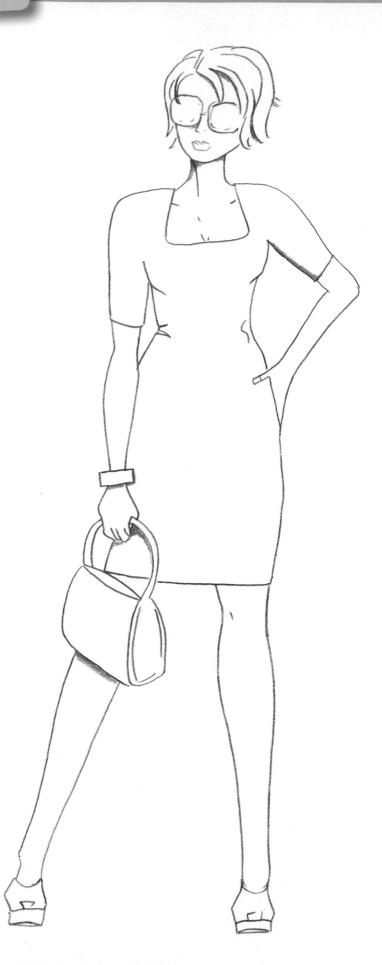

STEP 5 ▶

Add oversized sunglasses for
classic glamour, together with
a simple handbag and bangle.
Less is more with this look!

TOP TIP
A little creasing at the waist shows some movement in the fabric, but the key to this look is keeping the dress neat and simple.

STEP 6 ▶

Time for the ink. Working over the pencil, add thicker lines where the shadows will fall, around the neckline and at the waist.

STEP 7 ▶

The final step is adding the colour – black, of course, for the dress. Fuchsia-pink accessories make a stunning contrast and add a modern twist.

WHITE SHIRT

The white shirt, in all its different cuts and lengths, is a cool, classy addition to any girl's wardrobe. It looks great teamed with simple accessories and dark blue denim jeans.

 **◄ STEP 1**

Create your frame using clear lines to map out the figure. Draw your figure in a relaxed, straight-on pose.

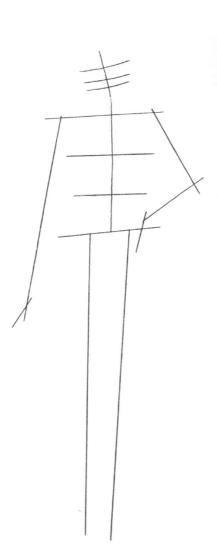

STEP 2 ►

Build your model's body structure on your line frame using cylinder and ball shapes.

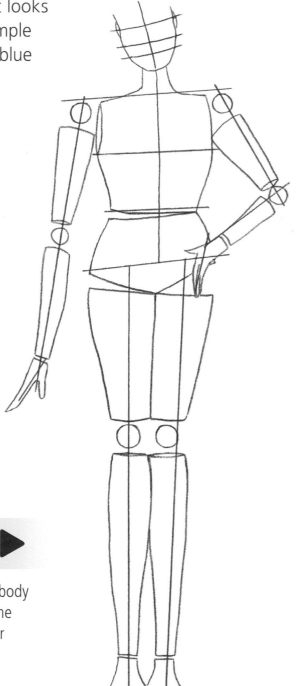

25

◀ STEP 3

Draw the outline of the garment. The shirt is fitted and has a nipped-in waist. Include up-to-date features such as oversized cuffs, collar and puffed sleeves. Keep the rest of the outfit simple by adding jeans and ballet pumps.

STEP 4 ▶

Add the facial features. For a casual, uncomplicated look, a long, flowing hairstyle works well.

TOP TIP

Make sure you are really happy with your pencil drawing before going over the lines in ink.

STEP 5 ▶

Add a pair of beaded hairclips with matching earrings, the shirt buttons and little bows on the ballet pumps. Add shading, particularly round the collar, cuffs and hem of the shirt.

STEP 6 ▶

Time to ink in your drawing.
Working over the pencil,
pay attention to areas of
shadow under the collar
and in the creases. Give
these a thicker line.

TOP TIP
Add interest by having
a hand-in-pocket
pose. The creasing
of the shirt above the
hand gives the fabric
movement.

STEP 7 ▶

Use a bright white for the shirt, adding some extra shading in pale grey. Colour the jeans in dark, indigo-blue and choose a nude shade for the pumps. Finish off your illustration with red lipstick and accessories.

Easy steps to...
creating a capsule wardrobe

You can put together a number of outfits from just a few key pieces in your wardrobe. Classic items are best, as they go easily with one another and do not date.

For a capsule wardrobe, it's best to keep the pieces fairly simple and choose complementary colours and styles so that you can mix and match.

Vest

Dress

Cropped denim jacket

Long-sleeved top

Skinny jeans

Scarf

Bag

Heels

Pumps

Skirt

**Just ten garments...
five fabulous outfits!**

TOP TIPS:

▶ Choose a base colour palette to suit your skin tone

▶ Choose an accent colour for accessories

▶ Choose clothes to suit your figure

▶ Go for classic items that will not date

▶ Mix and match to your heart's content!

PARTY WEAR

Parties are all about having fun and celebrating, and the three outfits in this chapter reflect that bubbly mood. These zingy, special-occasion pieces are fun both to wear and draw.

Sequinned Jacket

Shift Dress

Full Skirt

SHIFT DRESS

This gorgeous A-line shift dress is a modern reworking of a 1960s minidress. The perfect party piece – it's both easy to wear and high impact fashion.

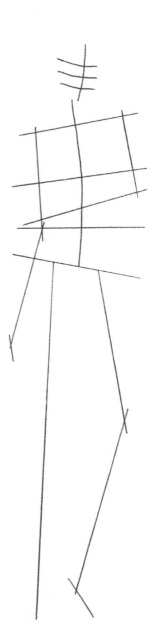

STEP 1 ▶

Create a frame for this relaxed pose using lines meeting at slight angles.

◀ STEP 2

Draw a figure from the basic shapes – cylinders for the limbs and torso, and balls for the joints.

STEP 3 ▶

Now draw the simple dress shape. Add a fabric panel feature just above the hem. High-heeled ankle boots complement the short length of the dress.

STEP 4 ▶

Remove your rough lines then add the hairstyle and facial details. A high, beehive hairstyle gives the model a retro look.

STEP 5 ▶

Next, add the accessories. We've chosen an oversized tote bag and long pendant necklace, both of which balance the shortness of the dress. Add a pair of sunglasses and gladiator-style boots to toughen up this girlie look.

TOP TIP
Copy the pose you want to draw, standing in front of a mirror. Use your reflection as a guide.

TOP TIP
Use a heavier ink line round the hem, down the length of the dress and round the bottom of the bag.

STEP 6 ▶

Use clean, precise ink lines for this outfit. Define the creases at the waist with a little heavier line work.

STEP 7 ▶

Colour the dress using bright orange – the quintessential 1960s colour. Cool the colour down with a cream feature panel at the hem and a cream pendant. This tangerine-dream dress looks great with dark chocolate-brown boots and bag.

FULL SKIRT

The party princess look is encapsulated in this full, knee-length satin skirt with net petticoat. Add diamante and sequins for extra sparkle and shine. This is a feminine, 1950s retro style.

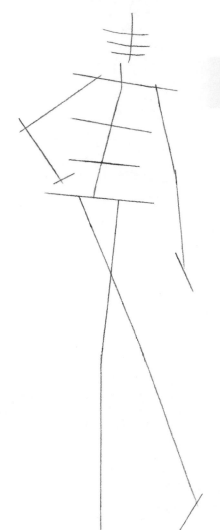

◀ STEP 1

This skirt needs to be modelled with a graceful pose. Start by creating a frame with softly curved outline.

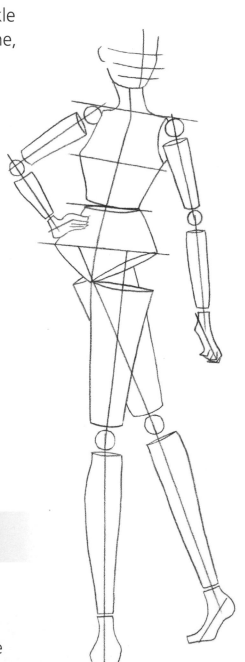

STEP 2 ▶

Build the body round the frame using cylinder and ball shapes. Make the figure tilt to one side slightly from the waist.

◀ **STEP 3**

Draw in the top and bias-cut skirt. The skirt is fitted at the waist, skims the hips, then flares out to the knee. Bias cut means that the pattern of the skirt is cut out on the fabric bias (along the diagonal).

STEP 4 ▶

Remove your working lines then add the facial features and a glamorous 'updo' hairstyle. A stiff underskirt of nylon net exaggerates the skirt's flare.

STEP 5 ▶

Now for the accessories! Add a bow belt and sequins to the satin overskirt to make it glitter. Ankle boots with a little fringe give a modern cow-girl twist. A studded clutch bag is a fun touch. Finish off with bracelets, a dress ring, and star-shaped pendant earrings.

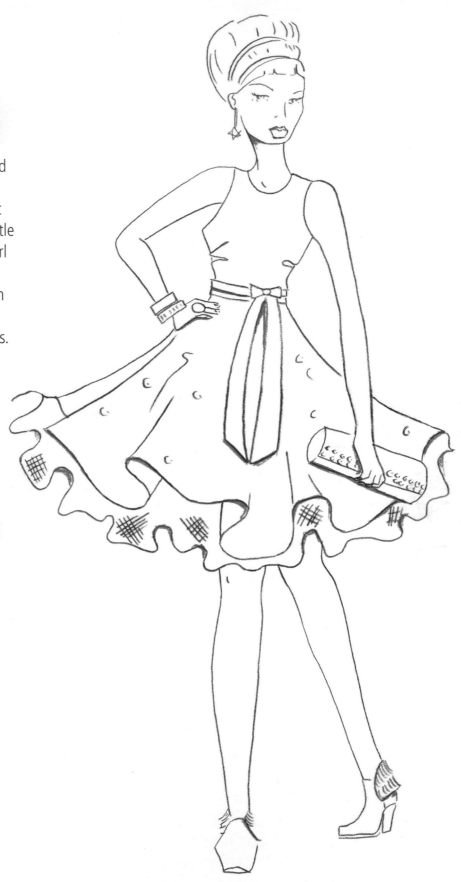

TOP TIP
Put a dark line of shading along the hem of the skirt to make the flare really stand out.

STEP 6 ▶

Now ink your drawing. Soft, fluid lines create an elegant look, and thicker lines give a fashion-sketch effect. Don't worry if you extend your lines a little, as it all adds to the sketchy feel.

PARTY WEAR

STEP 7 ▶

Now it's time for the colour.
Shades of pink, from pale
to shocking, make this a
super-girlie outfit and look
great teamed with silver-grey
accessories. Remember to
add some silver sparkle to
the sequins and jewellery.

SEQUINNED JACKET

This glittering statement jacket is all you need to turn a casual jeans and t-shirt look into a glamorous party outfit. Add gold accessories and heels and get ready to hit the dance floor!

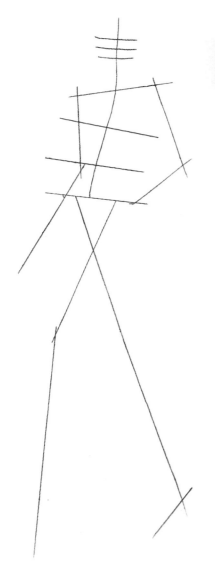

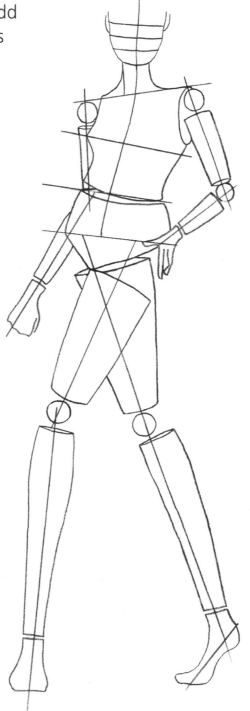

◀ STEP 1

Use your frame lines to create a figure with movement for this action pose.

STEP 2 ▶

Use the cylinder and ball method to build the body shape. Keep the figure relaxed, with a twist to the waist.

◀ STEP 3

Pencil in the shape of the outfit. The jacket is fitted at the waist and flares out at the hem. Add a simple t-shirt and skinny-fit jeans. Tuxedo lapels and high heels add a touch of glamour.

STEP 4 ▶

Add the facial features and hairstyle. A high ponytail gives the model more height and adds impact.

STEP 5 ▶

Time to add the accessories. Pencil in a leather clutch bag for carrying the party survival kit! Add a chunky bracelet and matching hoop earrings. Sequins scattered all over the heavyweight satin jacket give it glam-rock style.

TOP TIP
A good way to balance a high bun or ponytail is to give your model large earrings.

TOP TIP
Swing the hair out to one side to enhance the sense of movement.

STEP 6 ▶

To work up your ink, use thicker lines round the edge of the model and in the creases of the clothes to enhance the softness of the fabric.

STEP 7 ▶

For the colouring, a white
t-shirt and dark denim
jeans help make the jacket
stand out. The addition
of shiny accessories and
make-up are the finishing
touches to this party look.

Easy steps to...
party shoes

When planning what to wear, often it's best to start with the most important item – shoes, of course!

Shoes dictate the mood of an outfit. Once you've decided which pair to wear and your party feet are ready to hit the dance floor, the rest of the look just falls into place.

▲ **Peep-toe with bow**

▲ **Glitter pumps with flower detail**

▲ **Strappy sandals**

▲ **Shoe boots**

▲ **Gladiator sandals with heel**

Take five pairs of party shoes to create the perfect fun-time outfit!

Red accessories tie this look together

A simple dress with leggings looks great with the pumps

A short spaghetti-strapped party dress complements the gladiator sandals

A slinky, full-length dress is set off by the strappy sandals

For an ultra-feminine look, a prom-style dress is teamed with the peep-toed heels

ON LOCATION

Dressing up and acting a part embodies all that's fun and playful about fashion. The military, nautical and safari trends remain in vogue year after year.

Nautical Chic

Military Jacket

Safari Dress

MILITARY JACKET

The military jacket is a vital addition to any fashionista's wardrobe. Think buckles, shiny buttons and strong shoulders – structure and embellishment are the key to this piece. Keep the rest of the outfit simple and let the jacket do the talking.

STEP 1 ▶

This model needs a confident pose to show off the shape of the jacket. Create your frame using clear lines to map out the correct proportions.

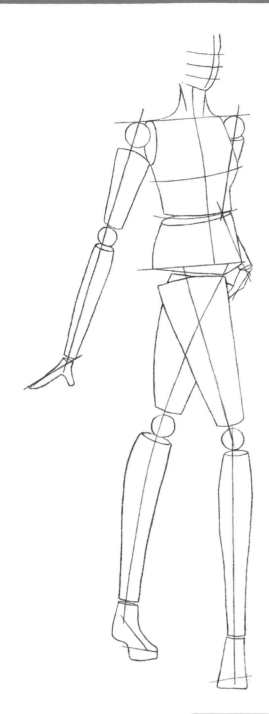

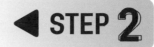 **STEP 2**

Build on your frame using basic shapes. The cylinder and ball method gives the figure structure and form.

STEP 3 ▶

Start to draw in the clothes. Keep the jacket cropped and nipped in at the waist. Team it with an oversized jumper for a modern, layered look. Add some chunky boots to emphasize the military theme.

STEP 4 ▶

Once you're happy with your drawing, rub out the pencil lines. Draw the facial features and a simple ponytail hairstyle to show off the structured shoulders of the jacket. Add the buttons and stitching.

STEP 5 ▶

Leather accessories work well with this look. Coordinate the messenger bag with the wide belt by giving them both a large buckle detail. Finish with some chunky jewellery.

TOP TIP
Try to press lightly with your pencil, so that mistakes are easier to rub out.

TOP TIP
Add creases to the jacket above and below the belt to define the model's waist.

STEP 6 ▶

The next step is to add the ink. Working over the pencil, pay attention to where the shadows should fall and ink these areas in a thicker line – for example, under the bag buckle and belt.

STEP 7 ▶

Finally add the colour. Choose neutral earthy colours, such as browns and greens, for your top and accessories so that the brightly coloured jacket is the showpiece. Finish off with classic blue denim jeans.

NAUTICAL CHIC

This outfit is perfect for holidays, summer shopping trips and meeting friends. The combination of red, white and blue is the key to this sailor-inspired theme. Add stripes, bows and nautical accessories to complete the look.

STEP 1 ▶

Use soft lines to create a relaxed pose for this outfit. Draw an open frame that will show off the stripes and other details.

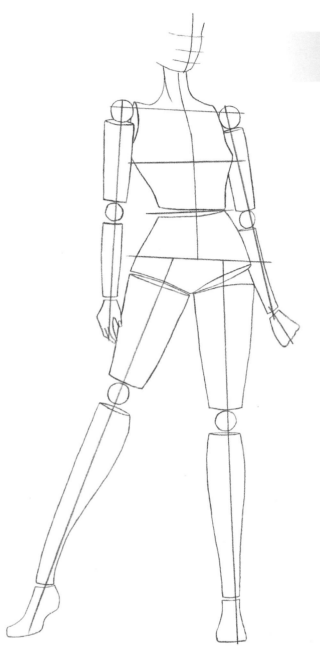

◀ **STEP 2**

Work up the pose using the basic shapes to fill out the body round the frame you have drawn.

STEP 3 ▶

Pencil in the outfit using clean lines. Keep the top tucked into the shorts to show off the high-waisted cut. Draw the outline for some simple ballet-pump shoes.

STEP 4 ▶

Add the features to the face and give the model luxuriant curly hair. Draw stripes on the top, then add stitching detail to the pockets on the shorts, and bows to the pumps.

STEP 5 ▶

Add accessories to complete the look. A pretty bow detail draws the eye to the off-the-shoulder top. Draw the bag and add an anchor trinket and rope handles. Pencil in a striped band in the hair and jumbo-sized buttons on the shorts. This is a busy look so keep the jewellery simple.

TOP TIP

If you are struggling to remember where to draw creases and folds, look in the mirror at your own clothes for reference.

STEP 6 ▶

Now start to ink your drawing. Keep an unstructured look to the fabric of the top. You can achieve this by drawing lines for the stripes that get thinner or disappear. Use slightly thicker lines under the buttons to make them stand out on the shorts.

TOP TIP

For each figure, start by choosing a pose that enhances the mood of the outfit.

STEP 7 ▶

Colour the final picture in red, white and blue. Complete the nautical effect with gold buttons, bag detail and jewellery, and beach-blonde hair.

SAFARI DRESS

This practical cotton dress, has been designed to keep the wearer cool without compromising on style. Team it with the right accessories and you've got a really hot look!

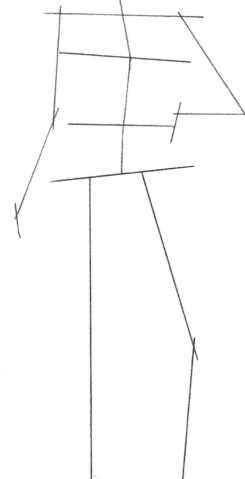

STEP 1 ▶

Use lines to create the body frame. Position a hand at the waist to give the figure a relaxed feel.

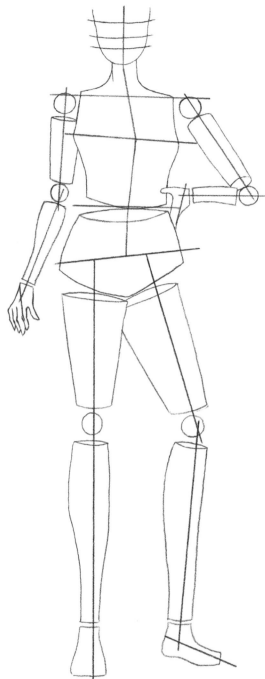

◄ STEP 2

Build your frame using the basic shapes. Push the model's hip out to the left to balance the bend in her leg.

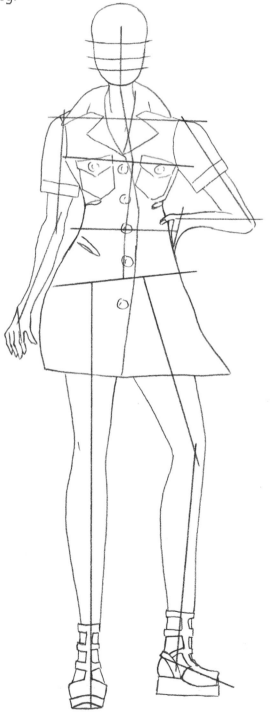

STEP 3 ▶

Pencil in the safari dress. To show movement from the hip, kick the skirt out to the right. Add patch pockets, buttons and gladiator-style sandals.

STEP 4 ▶

Add the facial features. A simple, short hairstyle works well with this outfit and sits neatly on the collar.

STEP 5 ▶

Large bangles and a wide belt add definition. A canvas clutch bag and bush hat work well with the safari theme. Oh, and don't forget the cool shades!

TOP TIP
Drawing hands can be difficult. Try gripping a purse with your own hand to work out the position of the fingers.

TOP TIP
Add plenty of shading round the collar and under the belt to create the impression of being out in the hot sun.

STEP 6 ▶

When inking in your pencil, use a thicker line round the belt and hat to make them stand out. Add crease lines round the pockets and buttons to create the feel of the crisp cotton fabric.

STEP 7 ▶

Khaki and sandy-gold colours work best for this outfit. Tie it all together with gold bangles and buckles. Colour the low wedge-heeled sandals in gold to complete the look.

Easy steps to...
theming your outfit

Create a number of looks and styles from one simple garment by adding accessories and changing hairstyle and make-up.

Smokey eye make-up with dark lips is great with this look

Add a simple band to pin up the hair and create the classic 20s bob

Add long gloves and a string of beads

▲ **Take a black shift dress...**

▲ **Elegant 20s**

Backcomb the hair for that 60s beehive and keep the make-up light in pastel colours with glossy lips

Go for a strong colour on the lips, with heavy eye make-up. Large hoop earrings are essential for gypsy chic

Leave hair loose and knot a silk scarf round the head

Big, bold beads are best for the 60s look

Pull on some over-the-knee socks

A bag with a large buckle completes the look

Take another scarf with tassel detail and tie at the waist

▲ Swinging 60s

▲ Gypsy chic

BEACH BABE

Floaty beach clothes are fantastic to wear, but the fabrics can be a challenge to draw. These outfits says sun, sand and summer. Follow the steps to create these three romantic, beach-chic looks.

MAXI DRESS

The maxi dress is a glamorous, relaxed and incredibly comfy addition to the beach wardrobe. Team it with oversized accessories for a sunny, beach babe feel.

STEP 1 ▶

Use lines to create a casual pose for your figure.

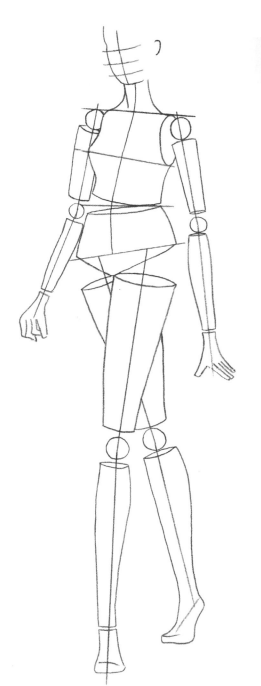

◀ STEP 2

Work up the pose, using the basic shapes of cylinder and ball to construct the body round the frame.

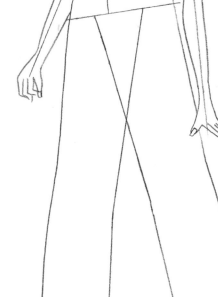

STEP 3 ▶

Add the long shape of the dress to the frame. The fabric is gathered under the bust, so add extra lines to this area. Add some classic strappy sandals.

STEP 4 ▶

Remove your working lines. Add facial features and draw the hairstyle. A long side-plait looks good and complements the long dress.

STEP 5 ▶

Now for the accessories! The length of the dress is balanced by an oversized shoulder bag. The beaded necklace and bracelet are fun, statement pieces. Draw some visor-style sunglasses as a finishing touch.

TOP TIP
Add lines all the way down the dress to show that the fabric is gathered.

TOP TIP

When colouring, add highlights to the dress where it would naturally catch the light.

STEP 6 ▶

Now it's time to ink your drawing. Use vertical lines for the gathers on the skirt of the dress. Make them thicker near the bodice and thinner towards the hem. Strong lines along the base of the bag and round the jewellery make these items stand out.

STEP 7 ▶

Finally, add the colour. Use a warm yellow for this sunny dress. Complement the yellow with tan accessories and dark sunglasses to complete this summery look.

KAFTAN AND BIKINI

An ultimate summer beach look, the bikini with kaftan is floaty and romantic yet practical. Whether lazing on a sun lounger or walking across the sand – you'll look great if you strike a pose in this outfit!

◀ **STEP 1**

Start by mapping out lines to create the model's walking pose.

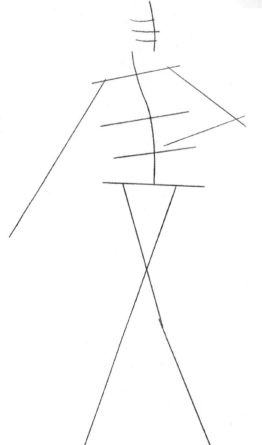

STEP 2 ▶

Build on your frame using the cylinder and ball shapes.

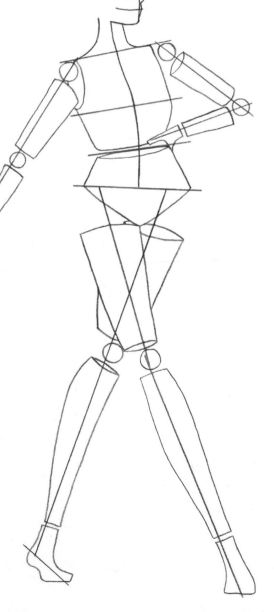

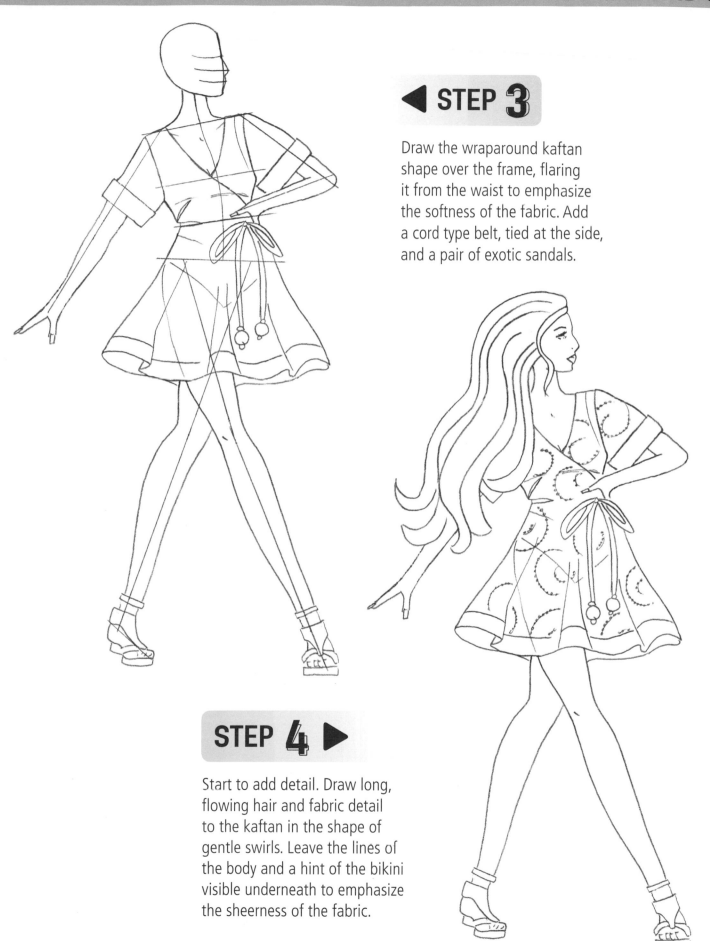

◀ STEP 3

Draw the wraparound kaftan shape over the frame, flaring it from the waist to emphasize the softness of the fabric. Add a cord type belt, tied at the side, and a pair of exotic sandals.

STEP 4 ▶

Start to add detail. Draw long, flowing hair and fabric detail to the kaftan in the shape of gentle swirls. Leave the lines of the body and a hint of the bikini visible underneath to emphasize the sheerness of the fabric.

STEP 5 ▶

Now add lots of accessories!
A large, statement necklace
works well, along with stacks
of bangles. Don't forget a pair
of shades, worn on the head.
A flower in the hair adds a
'boho' touch.

STEP 6 ▶

Draw a thick ink line round the bottom of the skirt to enhance the flare. Use subtle thin lines for the bikini just to give an impression of it.

TOP TIP
Make the kaftan fabric colours coordinate with the bikini and hair accessory.

STEP 7 ▶

Now colour your drawing. Sunshine yellow and clear aquamarine are the perfect beach colours for this outfit. They are set off by the dusky pink of the hair accessory to create a dreamy look.

PLAY SUIT

This youthful outfit is ideal for a day at the beach and is a chic alternative to summer skirts and dresses. The play suit looks great with huge beads and stripy wedged canvas sandals.

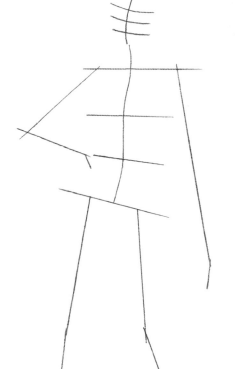

◀ **STEP 1**

This outfit requires a casual pose. Start with lines to create a relaxed looking framework.

STEP 2 ▶

Work up the body structure, using the cylinder shapes for limbs and torso and ball shapes for joints.

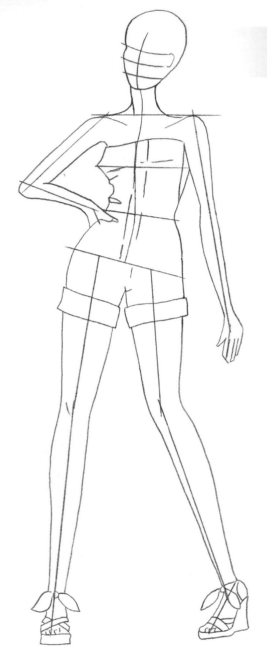

◀ **STEP 3**

Add the outline of the play suit, making sure it works with the body and pose. Pencil in the sandals, giving them bows at the ankles.

STEP 4 ▶

Sketch in the facial features and hairstyle. A high topknot looks cool and summery.

TOP TIP
Search clothes shops to find inspiration for different fabrics and prints.

STEP 5 ▶

Time to add the accessories. Oversized beads look good with the vintage style. Draw a ditzy floral print on the play suit and add a neat stripe to the sandals. A satchel worn across the body adds to the youthful look.

TOP TIP

Don't forget to add stitching detail to the bag. Small touches like this really help to lift your picture.

STEP 6 ▶

Time to ink your pencil. Use a heavy line round the underside of the jewellery and the bag. Thick lines round the play suit and thin lines for the floral print give the drawing definition.

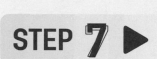

STEP 7 ▶

Now for the colour. Purple for the fabric background contrasts well with the bright orange floral pattern and jewellery. Finish the look with a tan satchel to complement the lightly tanned skin of the model.

Easy steps to . . . beach chic

With today's huge variety of fantastic accessories to choose from, looking great on the beach has never been easier. Here are just a few ways to enhance your beach-babe look.

The key to this look is relaxed, casual styling. Key beach-babe pieces are sunglasses, hair accessories and bags, with some pretty jewellery thrown in!

Sunglasses

Sunglasses are a beach essential. Here are three classic shapes. But there's no reason why a girl shouldn't have a different pair for every outfit!

Canvas

Over-the-shoulder

Wayfarers

Oversized

Aviators

Oversized

Beach bags

Whether you prefer a casual canvas bag, a smart over-the-shoulder purse, or an oversized shopper – a bag for keeping all your beach accessories in is a necessity. Go for a style that works well with your outfit.

Beach jewellery

There is lots of beach-inspired jewellery to choose from. Go for shells and spikey beads in lovely pastel colours for a natural look. Alternatively gold beads and bangles really stand out against lightly tanned skin.

Ankle bracelet

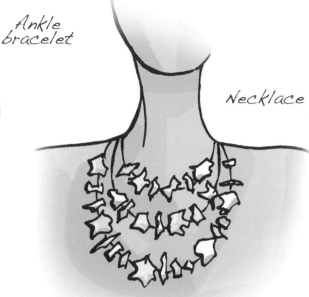

Necklace

Bangles

Beach hat

Headscarf

Hair braids

Head and hair accessories

For a relaxed look, loose hair under a headscarf tied in a side knot works well. Or, if you want something more classic, try a large floppy hat. Alternatively forget the headgear and work the hair – nothing says beach more than braids!

RED CARPET

A stunning red-carpet dress is often front page news. Colour, shape and style combine to produce the perfect dress, whether it is traditional, a little eccentric or just simply amazing!

FISHTAIL DRESS

To work the red carpet, you can't beat a fishtail dress. It is one of the most flattering outfits for a curvaceous figure. For this piece to shine, a movie starlet pose works best. So – head up, eyes forward, shoulders back, hand on hip… and smile!

STEP 1 ▶

Create your frame with straight lines, using a soft curve through the centre of the body.

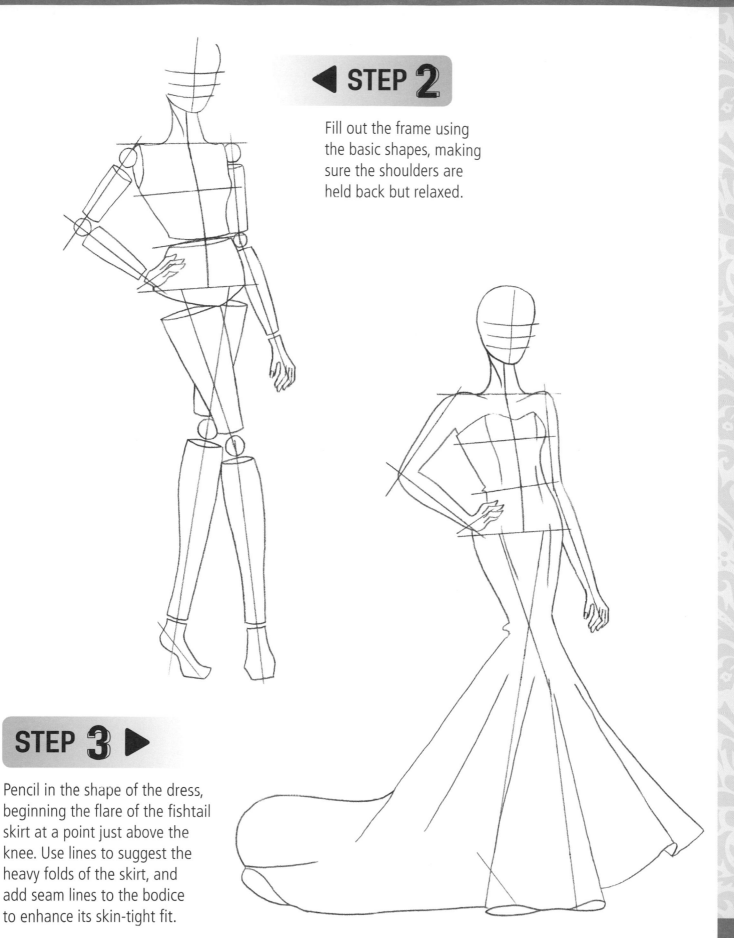

Fill out the frame using the basic shapes, making sure the shoulders are held back but relaxed.

STEP 3 ▶

Pencil in the shape of the dress, beginning the flare of the fishtail skirt at a point just above the knee. Use lines to suggest the heavy folds of the skirt, and add seam lines to the bodice to enhance its skin-tight fit.

STEP 4 ▶

Add facial features and the hairstyle. A soft chignon held at the side looks good, as it complements the sweetheart neckline of the dress.

STEP 5 ▶

Now it's time to add the accessories. A chunky clutch bag with matching bracelet keeps the look uncluttered. Hair accessories add interest, and a short pendant necklace works well, resting above the flattering neckline.

TOP TIP
Show the underside of the fabric round the hem to give the impression of volume.

TOP TIP
To emphasize the shiny fabric, draw a shadow down the skirt folds. Add highlights to show where light strikes the dress.

STEP 6 ▶

Start inking in your pencil. Use sweeping lines for the folds of the skirt and thicker lines to the outline of the dress.

STEP 7 ▶

Now for the colour – red and
black, a stunning combination!
What better way to make a
statement on the red carpet?

BANDAGE DRESS

The short special occasion dress needs to be particularly eye-catching to compete with all those elaborate, long red-carpet gowns out there. This figure-hugging number is glamorous and stylish. For the star who wants to be just that little bit different!

STEP 1 ▶

Create your body frame using straight lines for the arms and legs, making a soft curve for the torso.

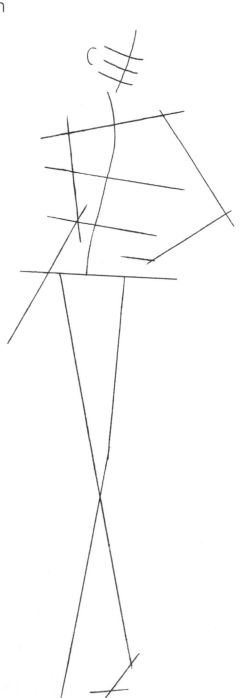

◀ STEP 2

Build the pose using the basic shapes and keeping the body curve soft and fluid.

STEP 3 ▶

Pencil in the dress on your body shape. Make sure the seams work with the curve of the pose. Add peep-toed court shoes for height and elegance.

STEP 4 ▶

Add the facial details and hairstyle. Keeping the hair long and loose works well with the shortness of the dress. Rub out the rough pencil lines and check that your dress looks stretchy and figure-hugging.

TOP TIP
Don't worry if your lines aren't precise. You can improve them at the inking stage.

STEP 5 ▶

Now add some evening accessories: a bold oversized bracelet, hoop earrings and a purse with a beaded handle.

STEP 6 ▶

When inking in your model, use a heavier line down one side of the body to enhance the pose. Add small lines for the creases to emphasize the stretch and softness of the fabric.

TOP TIP

When inking in the seams of the dress, start with a thick line and make it gradually thinner to give the model a 3-D appearance.

STEP 7 ▶

Now for the colour. Two-tone purple works well for this bandage-style design. Add dark hair and olive skin, for an overall sultry effect.

BACKLESS DRESS

The long backless dress is often spotted on the red carpet. It is all draping and elegance and requires a special stance. The best pose to show off this dress has the model turning her head to glance over one shoulder, while leaning backwards slightly.

STEP 1 ▶

Create a frame for the body, using straight lines and a soft curve for the spine running from the neck to the hips.

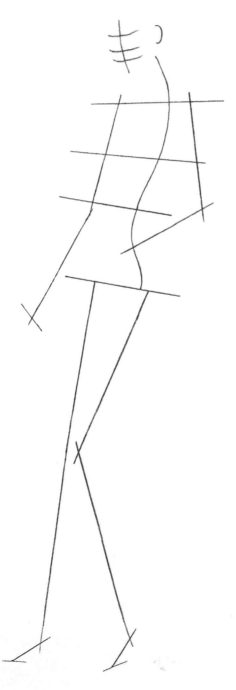

STEP 2

Build the body using your basic cylinder and ball shapes, making sure the model is balanced on her outstretched leg to keep the pose looking comfortable.

STEP 3 ▶

Pencil in the dress, making it narrow between hips and knee and flaring out towards the hem. Draw curved lines at the small of the back for the draped section and give the dress a small train for added glamour.

STEP 4 ▶

Add the facial features and hair. A short, mussed-up hairstyle contrasts well with the sleekness of the long dress.

STEP 5 ▶

So that attention is not drawn away from the dress, keep the accessories simple. An oversized ring on the finger and large hoop earrings are sufficient. A necklace would break up the continuity of the backless feature.

TOP TIP
Shade the gathered layers to give the appearance of depth to the fabric.

TOP TIP
Use solid inking in the centre of the earrings to give them a sense of weight.

STEP 6 ▶

Ink the dress in with thick sweeping lines down its length to create the look of heavy fabric falling into folds. Add thick lines round the draped section at the small of the back to enhance this feature.

STEP 7 ▶

The midnight blue colour of this dress contrasts brilliantly with the pale skin of the model. As the fabric is so dark, you need to add plenty of highlights to accentuate the glossy eveningwear look. Make the jewellery a bronze colour to complement the dark blue and give the model light, luminous make-up.

Easy steps to . . . Hollywood glamour

How to achieve all-out red carpet glamour.

▼ Chiffon layers

This dress is soft and floaty and works well in pastel colours.

▼ Romantic ruffles

With its long flounced skirt, this dress moves beautifully as you walk. It works well in a dark grey colour.

The perfect make-up here is pastel shades with highlights on the eyelids

Give this dress even more feminine style with a pretty evening bag

Soft eye make-up with a strong lip colour works well with this dress

Two dramatic pieces of jewellery are sufficient to set off this flamboyant gown

▼ Silky and smooth

This lovely fitted dress flares out from the knee. A slinky garment, it works well in deep purple.

▼ Oversized bow

This sharp, simple dress works well in black and white.

Keep the make-up classic and simple for this style of dress

A jewelled hairslide and pendant earrings add more glamour

Draw attention to the eyes by using dark eyeshadow and keeping the lips pale

Add extra bling with a bejewelled clutch bag

Use lots of dramatic make-up on the eyes and lips for this dress

Add an oversized bracelet to balance the oversized bow

▶ Gathers and pleats

A fitted bodice with a dramatic gathered skirt works well in a deep red fabric that catches the light.

Accessorize with plenty of bling - big earrings with matching necklace and a dress ring. Clip up the gathers of the skirt with a large jewelled brooch

DESIGN ICONS

Catwalk fashions are created by designers, some of whom are so influential that they have become household names. Here are three such design icons whose styles have influenced generations of women.

Coco Chanel

Vivienne Westwood

Christian Dior

VIVIENNE WESTWOOD

Vivienne Westwood is renowned for her eccentric, British-inspired pieces. She shot to fame in 1981 with a colourful, romantic collection based on a pirate theme. Today she is one of the world's leading fashion designers.

STEP 1 ▶

This pose needs a lot of attitude. Start with clean lines to create the frame of a straight-on pose.

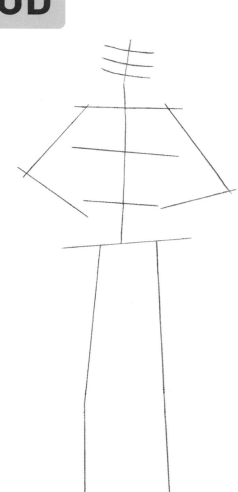

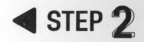 **STEP 2**

Use cylinders and balls to fill out the body around the frame.

STEP 3 ▶

Create the basic shape of the outfit using clean lines. The exaggerated structure of the dress is emphasized by a tight corset top, a motif often used by Westwood. Another of her instantly recognizable creations is the oversized platform shoe.

STEP 4 ▶

Pencil in the facial features and the hair. Little kiss curls in a big hairstyle work well. Westwood designs her garments with a rebellious twist, often using traditional fabrics. She is famous for using more than one tartan print in the same outfit.

STEP 5 ▶

Just one tartan is used here, but it's combined with a delicate mesh underskirt for an unconventional look. Accessorize this outfit with a bold necklace and earrings for style that packs a punch!

TOP TIP

Show mesh or net fabric by drawing soft criss-crossed lines in pencil.

TOP TIP
Keep the lines on the tartan light and fluid so they follow the shape of the dress on the body.

STEP 6 ▶

Time to work with the ink. Use thick lines round the outline of the dress. Pay particular attention to the pleats on the skirt and round the buttons to make them really stand out and illustrate the heaviness of the fabric. In contrast, use light thin lines for the mesh underskirt.

STEP 7 ▶

For the colour, a red-based tartan with dark green detail works well. Matching thick green tights complete the Westwood look.

CHRISTIAN DIOR

Christian Dior achieved world fame with his creative shapes and silhouettes. Working in post-war France, Dior reacted against the fabric shortages of the time by using up to 20 yards of luxurious fabric for an outfit. His styling has influenced other designers ever since.

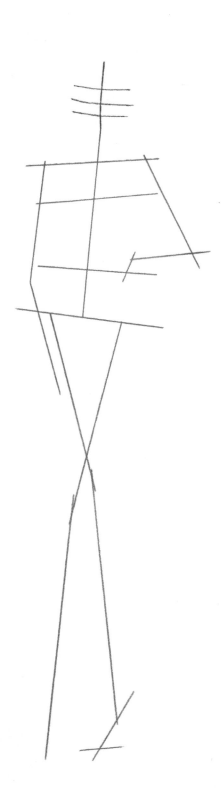

STEP 1 ▶

Use straight lines for this pose. The model needs to stand tall, with her head held high.

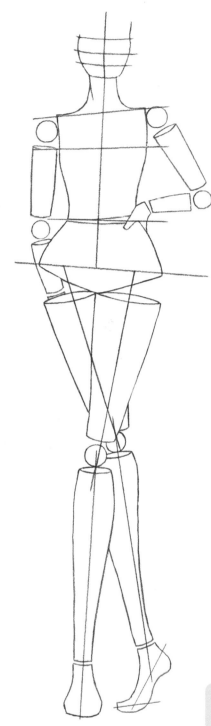

◀ STEP 2

Using the basic shapes, create the elegant pose around the frame. Use balls for the joints and cylinders for the limbs and torso.

STEP 3 ▶

Pencil in the dress. To make a strong silhouette, draw the skirt pulled in to a tiny waist and flaring out at the hem. Add an underskirt to exaggerate the flare. Add a classic pair of court shoes.

STEP 4 ▶

Remove your working lines then pencil in the facial features and the hair. An updo hairstyle works well with this piece. Keep it restrained and sophisticated so that the focus remains on the silhouette of the dress.

STEP 5 ▶

Now for the accessories. Add a pillbox hat on the side of the head. Pearl jewellery and a narrow belt complete the look. Don't forget the beautiful ultra-long gloves — no elegant lady would be seen without them!

TOP TIP
Use curved lines to enhance the shape of the skirt.

STEP 6 ▶

Using your finished pencil as a guide, start to work on the ink. Use a heavy line where there is more shadow – on the underskirt, for example. This will maximize the flared look.

TOP TIP

When adding the colour, use large amounts of highlight to make the skirt really stand out.

STEP 7 ▶

Working with the colour, use a sophisticated chartreuse yellow for the bodice and overskirt, with a soft silver grey for the underskirt and gloves. Use black detailing to accentuate the shoulders and waist.

COCO CHANEL

Coco Chanel is renowned for combining elegance, sophistication and originality. One of her most famous pieces is her trademark two-piece suit. With a few variations over the years, this classic garment has remained in fashion since Chanel created it in the 1920s.

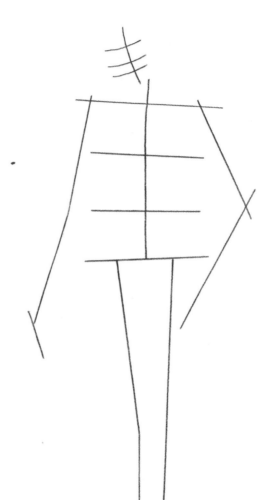

STEP 1 ▶

Use straight lines to create a straight-on pose. Tilt the head slightly for a demure 1950s look.

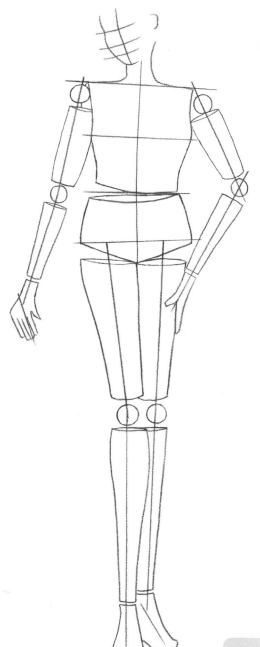

◀ STEP **2**

Use cylinder and ball shapes to build the structure around the frame.

STEP **3** ▶

Now draw your suit on to the body shape. Add creases at the waist and elbows to show the softness of the fabric. Draw in the pocket flaps and the suit jacket trim. The jacket is teamed with a pencil skirt.

STEP 4 ▶

Remove your working lines, then add buttons, facial features and the hair. An elegant updo works well with this style and will fit neatly underneath the hat.

STEP 5 ▶

Time to add the accessories. Pearl earrings and matching necklace, a shallow, flat-brimmed hat and gloves with matching trim. Lastly, add Chanel's trademark quilted purse.

TOP TIP
Draw the head angled down and to one side to give the model a demure look.

TOP TIP

Don't forget to add thicker lines to the quilting detail of the purse to emphasize its shape.

STEP 6 ▶

Now start to work with the ink. Illustrate shadow by using plenty of thick lines round the outline of the suit, under the pocket flaps and in the creases.

STEP 7 ▶

Now for the colour. Use a cream base for this outfit, setting it off with black trim, buttons, bag and pearls. Black-and-cream brogue style shoes create an elegant, businesslike effect.

Easy steps to...
designing your own clothes

Customizing your clothes and breathing new life into old garments is easier than you think! Here are five top tips to get you started.

Transforming old jeans into a denim skirt!

STEP 1 ▼

Take an old pair of jeans.

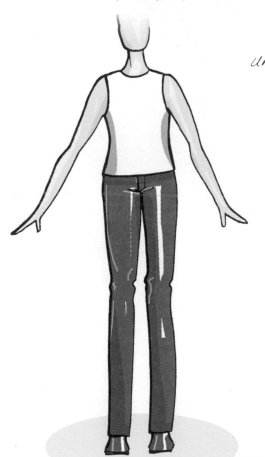

STEP 2 ▼

Unpick the inside leg at the front and back then cut off the legs at the length you want.

Unpick the seams

Cut off the legs

STEP 3 ▼

Sew the inside front of the left leg to the inside front of the right leg. Do this at the front and back.

sew the material together

STEP 4 ▼

Your new skirt is complete!

Customizing clothes

Reinvent an item of clothing by adding buttons, ribbons, sequins, bows, chains or feathers.

STEP 1 ▲

Take a plain vest top.

STEP 2 ▲

Measure your chosen trimmings by loosely draping them across the front of the vest.

STEP 3 ▲

Use a needle and thread to sew the ends of the chains at the neck/shoulder seams. Then attach an oversized bow to the front of the vest.

Other fun ideas to try:

Transfer printing

Take a plain t-shirt

Use an iron-on transfer print to transform it!

Super-long scarf

How about learning to knit? It's not just for grannies!

Circular skirt

Cut a circle from a piece of fabric. Make a hole the size of your waist in the circle. With a needle and thread, stitch a waistband of fabric-covered elastic round the hole. Now put the skirt on . . . and twirl!